PART ONE

HITLER'S DICTATORSHIP

Heil Hitler! The scene from inside Adolf Hitler's car
as he drove through Berlin after coming to power on 30 January 1933

Imagine that you are German, that you are walking along a street in Germany fifty years ago, and that you recognise a group of people walking towards you. This is what a German newspaper of 1936, *Schwarzes Korps*, says you should do:

> 'If people belong to the same social group, it is customary to raise the right arm at an angle so that the palm of the hand becomes visible. The appropriate phrase that goes with it is "Heil Hitler" or at least "Heil". If one person meets a person socially – or through any other circumstances – inferior to oneself, then the right arm is to be fully stretched out, raised to eye level; at the same time, one is to say "Heil Hitler". The greeting should always be carried out with the left arm if one's right arm is engaged by a lady.'

If you are the kind of person who likes a quiet life, you will always follow these rules when you see people you

know; there is always a chance that one of them will report you to the Gestapo – the secret police – if you do not give the 'German greeting' and say 'Heil Hitler'.

To be really sure of a quiet life, you will be a member of the National Socialist German Workers' Party – the Nazi Party for short. You will have a copy of Adolf Hitler's book *Mein Kampf* out on the table when friends or neighbours visit your home. You might think of hanging a framed portrait of Adolf Hitler above the mantlepiece. And you will certainly never say anything against him in public, for he is the dictator of Germany and does not allow any kind of opposition.

This book invites you to discover how one man was able to get such total control over sixty million Germans that they saluted each other and said his name whenever they met. Let us begin by deciding what kind of man he was.

1

ADOLF HITLER

Hitler (right) with fellow soldiers in 1916

His life up to 1933

1889 – 1909

Adolf Hitler was born in 1889 in Braunau, a small town in Austria. His parents paid for him to go to a special High School, hoping that he would qualify for a good job. But he failed his examinations and left school at sixteen. For the next two years he did not work, but read books, listened to music and painted pictures. At nineteen he left home and went to Vienna, the capital of Austria, to be an art student. But the Art Academy there did not want him. Without qualifications and without a job, he ended up living in a hostel for tramps.

1909 – 13

After being rejected by the Vienna Art Academy, Hitler had to make a living in any way he could. He did odd jobs – cleaning carpets or sweeping snow in the winter – and he painted postcards to sell in the streets. During his five years in Vienna he became interested in politics. He supported nationalist parties which wanted to make Austria more powerful, and he grew to hate socialist parties which were demanding better wages, better conditions and the right to vote for working people. He also came to hate people of foreign races, especially Jewish people. He thought that foreigners were ruining the life and culture of his country.

1913 – 18

Hitler left Austria in 1913 to get out of doing national service in the army. He went to live in Munich in Germany. He was not a coward, however, for he volunteered to join the German army as soon as the First World War began in 1914. For the whole of the war he was on active service, doing the dangerous job of taking messages between the trenches. He was wounded twice, once by rifle fire and once by poison gas. He won six medals for bravery, including the Iron Cross First Class, the highest award a German soldier could win. Corporal Hitler said that the war was 'the greatest of all experiences' and was bitter and angry when Germany surrendered in 1918. He blamed the surrender on Jews and on socialist politicians.

1918 – 23

Hitler stayed in the army after the war was over. He worked as a 'V man', spying on political parties to find out if they were dangerous. One party he spied upon, the German Workers Party, was not at all dangerous, for it had only a few members and funds of only 7.5 marks – about £2. But he liked its ideas and joined it in 1919. Before long Hitler was leader of the party which he renamed the National Socialist German Workers Party – **Nazi Party** for short. He made the swastika, the crooked cross, the symbol of the party. He organised 'Storm Troopers' in brown uniforms to beat up people who disagreed with him – especially Socialists and Communists. He held meetings at which he made powerful speeches, saying that Germany needed a strong leader, that Germany must get revenge for her defeat in the war, and that Jews and Communists were 'germs' that must be destroyed.

1923 – 33

In 1923 Hitler and his Storm Troopers tried to overthrow the government by starting a *putsch*, an attempt to get power by force, in Munich. They failed and Hitler was put in prison for high treason. While in prison he wrote a book about his life and his ideas called *Mein Kampf* – My Struggle. He was let out of prison after only a year and went back to running the Nazi Party. For four years he had little success, but in 1929 an economic depression hit Germany. Unemployment shot up to six million. People without jobs began to listen to Hitler's ideas about strong leadership and, like him, many blamed Jews and communists for their unemployment. More and more people voted for the Nazis in elections until they became Germany's biggest party. After two landslide victories in elections in 1932, Hitler became Chancellor of Germany in January 1933.

Hitler in 1931, wearing Storm Trooper uniform, inspecting an SA unit

His ideas

Most of Hitler's ideas can be found in *Mein Kampf*, the book which he wrote in prison in 1924. It is very long and boring to read, but it does tell us in detail about his ideas, so it is very useful to historians. This is a summary of the ideas in the book:

The Fuehrer principle

Germany must be ruled by a single, strong leader who has great power – a 'Fuehrer'.

Lebensraum (living space)

Germans need more land to live and work in. They will get this extra land by taking over countries east of Germany – Poland and Russia, for example. They will use force to get this land if the eastern countries do not give it up.

Race

Human beings are divided into races. Some races are better than others. The best races are 'pure' ones which have not interbred with others. The Germans, who belong to the 'Aryan' race must keep themselves pure in order to become the 'master race'.

Anti-semitism

Jews, or Semites as Hitler called them, are the biggest threat to the purity of the Germans. They are also involved in a great conspiracy to take control of the world. They helped to bring about Germany's defeat in the Great War. Jews must therefore be destroyed.

Communism

Communism, the political system of Russia, is dangerous, so it too must be destroyed.

The Treaty of Versailles

The peace treaty which Germany signed in 1919 is unfair. It must be cancelled and the land which it took away from Germany must be returned. France must be destroyed.

His appeal

What attracted people to Hitler and the Nazi Party? Albert Speer, a leading Nazi, described what he felt after hearing a speech by Hitler in 1931:

> 'Here it seemed to me was hope. Here were new ideals, a new understanding, new tasks. The perils of Communism could be checked, Hitler persuaded us, and instead of hopeless unemployment, Germany could move towards economic recovery. . . . It must have been during these months that my mother saw a Storm Trooper parade in the streets of Heidelburg. The sight of discipline in a time of chaos, the impression of energy in an atmosphere of universal hopelessness, seems to have won her over also.'

Many people at the time commented that Hitler could hypnotise audiences when he made speeches. An American journalist described how:

> 'When, at the climax [*of a speech*] he sways from one side to the other his listeners sway with him; when he leans forward and when he ends they are either awed or silent or on their feet in a frenzy.'

Work section

A. Test your understanding of what you have read by explaining each of the following words: Nazi Party, swastika, Fuehrer, *lebensraum*, anti-semitism, Aryan.

B. Make a time-chart of events in Hitler's life from 1889 up to 1933. You should be able to find ten important events in this chapter.
Example:
1889: Born in Braunau, a small town in Austria.
If you find out about other events from different books, add them to your time-chart.

C. Study Albert Speer's account of his feelings after hearing a speech by Hitler in 1931. What reasons did he give for supporting the Nazi party?

THE ROAD TO DICTATORSHIP

Hitler became Chancellor – Prime Minister – of Germany on 30 January 1933. Eighteen months later he was a dictator with total power.

Obstacles

His first steps on the road to dictatorship were the most difficult. Germany was a democracy, so Hitler could only make laws if parliament – the **Reichstag** – agreed to them. But more than half the seats in the Reichstag belonged to parties which opposed him. Somehow he would have to get rid of these, particularly the Socialists and Communists who were his main opponents.

A second difficulty was that Hitler owed his job to Germany's President, General von Hindenburg. Just as Hindenburg had made Hitler Chancellor, so he could make him resign if he thought Hitler was not governing the country properly. Hitler therefore had to be very careful about the way he got rid of his opponents in the Reichstag.

The elections of March 1933

Hitler arranged for a general election to be held in March 1933. He hoped that the Nazi Party would win a landslide victory and get a majority of the seats in the Reichstag. A week before voting day, the Reichstag building went up in flames. A Communist, Marianus van der Lubbe, was caught on the scene with matches and fire-lighters in his pockets. Hitler said this was the start of a Communist plot to take over the country. He went to President Hindenburg and asked him to make a special law, the **Law for the Protection of the People and State**. Hindenburg had the power to make new laws in an emergency, even if the Reichstag did not agree, and he believed Hitler's claim that Germany was in a state of emergency. He made the law that Hitler wanted, not realising that it would help Hitler become a dictator.

The new law banned Communists and Socialists from taking part in the election campaign. Four thousand of them were thrown into prison, their newspapers were shut down, and Nazi Storm Troopers (*Sturmabteilung* – **SA**) beat up their supporters in the streets.

As a result of banning the Communists, Hitler and the Nazis won just under half the vote. It was not the majority that Hitler wanted, but it was enough to persuade the new Reichstag to agree to an **Enabling Law** on 23 March 1933. This let Hitler make laws without asking the Reichstag for its consent.

Now Hitler could do what he liked to his opponents without having to worry about what Hindenburg thought of him.

Germany becomes a one-party state

Hitler used the power of the Enabling Law to get rid of anything or anyone that limited his authority. On 7 April 1933 he put Nazi officials in charge of the local governments which ran Germany's provinces. On 2 May he closed down trade unions, took away their funds and put their leaders in prison. Then, on 14

Armed Nazi Storm Troopers arrest Communists during the election campaign of March 1933

July, he made a **Law against the Formation of New Parties**. This said that the Nazi Party was the only party allowed to exist in Germany: anyone trying to set up or run another party would be punished with three years hard labour. In this way Germany became a one party state.

The Nazi Party had millions of members and many thousands of officials. It was organised very carefully so that every German citizen could be kept under their control, even if they were not members. This diagram shows how the system worked:

The structure of the Nazi Party
Adolf Hitler, leader of the Party

gave orders to   reported to

42 *Gauleiters* (district leaders). A *Gau*, or area, was a province of the country

gave orders to   reported to

760 *Kreisleiters* (area leaders). A *Kreis* was a subdivision of a *Gau*

gave orders to   reported to

21, 354 *Ortsgruppefuehrer* (local group leaders)

gave orders to   reported to

70, 000 *Zellenleiters* (cell leaders). In charge of town suburbs

400, 000 *Blockleiters* (block leaders). Each in charge of one block of flats or group of houses

---

The block leaders, although they were lowest in the party structure, had the most important job to do – snooping on their neighbours. By listening to the local gossip, and even by listening at keyholes, they could find out who were the grumblers, critics, and petty criminals and report them to their superiors in the party. And that meant getting into trouble with the police, for, as we shall see, the Nazi Party controlled the police force of Germany.

The 'Night of the Long Knives'

Hitler had made Germany into a one party state, but he soon had problems to deal with in the Nazi Party itself. Two million party members were Storm Troopers, the thugs who had smashed the Communists during the 1933 elections. Their leader, **Ernst Roehm**, wanted to make them part of the German army. This alarmed Hitler, for it would make Roehm the most powerful man in Germany. The army generals did not like the idea either. They were busy building up the strength of the army and, as one of them said later, 'rearmament was too serious a business and tricky to allow thieves, drunks and sods to be involved'.

At three in the morning of 30 June 1934, Roehm and the other SA leaders were arrested on Hitler's orders, taken to prison, and shot. Over the next few days, some 400 people were executed in this way. The killings were done by Hitler's own black shirted guards, the **SS** (*Schutzstaffel*, or Protection Squads).

Hitler becomes Fuehrer

One month after the SA leaders had been butchered by the SS, President Hindenburg died, aged 87. Hitler immediately took over the Presidency and gave himself the title '**Fuehrer and Reich Chancellor**'. On the same day, 2 August 1934, the officers and men of the army swore the following oath:

> 'I will render unconditional obedience to the Fuehrer of the German Reich and people, Adolf Hitler, the supreme commander of the armed forces, and will be ready as a brave soldier to stake my life at any time for this oath.'

The only Germans with the power to oppose Hitler, soldiers with guns, had sworn their lives away to him.

Work section

A. Test your understanding of this chapter by explaining each of the following terms: Chancellor, Reichstag, Enabling Law, one party state, Gauleiters, block leaders.

B. Explain how Hitler increased his power on each of the following dates: 23 March 1933, 7 April 1933, 2 May 1933, 14 July 1933, 30 June 1934, 2 August 1934. Do this in table form. Example:

Date	Event	How it increased Hitler's power
23 March 1933	The Enabling Law was passed.	Hitler was now able to make laws without asking for the consent of the Reichstag.

C. Examine the photograph on the opposite page.
  1. What law allowed the Storm Troopers to do this to opponents of the Nazi Party?
  2. Why would you call this situation unfair, even though it was allowed by law?

D. Make revision notes on what you have read so far, using points A and B of the revision guide on page 20 to help you.

THE NAZI POLICE STATE

All dictators risk being overthrown by their opponents. Dictators therefore need large police forces to protect them. For this reason a dictatorship is often called a police state. This chapter shows you how Hitler's police state was organised.

The most important job of any police force is to investigate crimes and then to catch the people who have committed them. The police in Nazi Germany were different: their job was to arrest people before they committed crimes.

The method was simple. All local police units had to draw up lists of people who might be 'Enemies of the State'. They gave these lists to the **Gestapo**, the Secret State Police. This organisation was a branch of the SS, and it had the power to do exactly as it liked.

Imagine that your name is on a list of 'Enemies of the State'; this is what is likely to happen to you. You

Germany's police chiefs: left, Heinrich Himmler,
Reichfuehrer *SS and Chief of German Police; right,*
Reinhard Heydrich, Chief of the Gestapo, and Himmler's
second in command

are woken at three in the morning by a violent knocking at the door. When you open it, two men in black uniforms tell you that you have three minutes to pack a bag. Then they take you to the nearest police station where you are shut in a cell.

Some time later – it may be days, weeks or months – you are brought up from the cells and told to sign Form D-11, an 'Order for Protective Custody'. By signing it, you are agreeing to go to prison, but you are too scared to refuse to sign it. Without being given a trial you are then taken to a **concentration camp** where you will stay for as long as the Gestapo pleases.

How have you come to be in this terrible situation? A former prisoner of Buchenwald concentration camp described to the British Foreign Office in 1939 the kinds of people who ended up there in 'protective custody':

A. 'How is the population of a concentration camp in present-day Germany brought together? In Buchenwald there were 8000 of us, 2000 Jews and 6000 non-Jews.

Our 8000 prisoners included first of all the "politicals" (as, for example, the Communist members of the Reichstag), many of whom have been in various concentration camps ever since 1933. . . . In addition to the genuine political prisoners there are many poor devils at Buchenwald accused of having spoken abusively of the sacred person of the Fuehrer. . . .

After the "political", the category of the so-called "work-shy" is the largest. Anyone who imagines that this group has to do with tramps and vagabonds is grossly deceived. An example. A business employee lost his position and applied for unemployment relief. One fine day he was informed by the Labour Exchange that he could obtain employment as a navvy on the new motor roads. This man, who was looking for a commercial post, turned down the offer. The Labour Exchange then reported him to the Gestapo as being "work-shy", and he was then arrested and sent to a concentration camp.

The next group were the "*Bibelforscher*" a religious sect taking its doctrine from the bible. . . but proscribed [*banned*] by the Gestapo since its members refuse military service.

The fourth category consisted of the homosexuals. . . . To charge those it dislikes with this offence is a favourite tactic of the secret police. . . .

The last class of prisoners were the professional criminals. . .'

Roll-call in Oranienburg concentration camp, Berlin, in April 1933

The concentration camps were run by another branch of the SS, the **Deaths Head Units**, who wore skull and crossbone badges on their uniforms. This account, by 'Herr X', of how they treated prisoners was written down for him in 1938 by a charity organisation working in Germany:

B. 'Herr X, a well-to-do Jewish business man, was for six weeks in the concentration camp at Buchenwald. . . . Herr X said that the working hours were sixteen per day, Sundays and week-days alike. During these hours it was forbidden to drink, even in the hottest weather. The food in itself was not bad, but quite insufficient. Weak coffee at dawn and a half litre of soup at midday; bread allowance for the whole day 250 grammes. . . . While he was there the work of the Jewish prisoners was doubled, and their rations halved. The work, of course, consists of moving heavy stones, often far beyond the strength of a normal well-fed man.

The men were kept standing to attention for many hours on end. Floggings were very frequent, for such small offences as drinking water during working hours. The usual punishment was twenty-five strokes given alternately by two guards. This often produced unconsciousness, but the Jews were told that the Fuehrer had himself given orders that the Jews might receive up to sixty strokes.

Herr X was in a group of 480 men who had only one tap at which to wash and drink for a quarter of an hour on getting up. Later even this was stopped. During the six weeks he was in the camp, Herr X saw neither soap nor toothbrush.

Deaths took place daily in the camp. (Their relatives were often first informed of this by a call from an official who said they could have the ashes on payment of three marks). . .'

Work section

A. Test your understanding of this chapter by explaining what each of the following means: Gestapo, Protective Custody, concentration camps, Deaths Head Units.

B. Study document A on the opposite page. Make a detailed list of the kinds of people who were likely to be arrested as 'Enemies of the State' in Nazi Germany.

C. 1. Judging by the evidence of document B, above, what do you think were the purposes of concentration camps?
2. Suggest why the prisoners were treated so badly.

D. Study the photograph above, noting the date when it was taken.
1. For what reason might the people have been imprisoned in the concentration camp?
2. How long do you think they have been in this camp?
3. What sort of experiences do you think they have had since being arrested?

4

THE JEWS IN NAZI GERMANY
1933 – 1939

The people who suffered most under Nazi rule were Jews. As you have found out, Hitler hated Jewish people. He believed that they were to blame for Germany's defeat in the Great War and that Jewish businessmen were plotting to take control of the world. Hitler also believed that the Jews were an 'inferior race' and should not be allowed to mix with the 'superior' Aryan Germans. So, once in power, Hitler quickly began to make life difficult for them. The SA, the Storm Troopers, organised a boycott of Jewish shops, while Jews were sacked from important jobs in the civil service, the law, universities and schools, broadcasting and newspapers.

Next, in 1934, all Jewish shops were marked with a yellow star or with the word '*Juden*', German for 'Jews'. In parks and on buses and trains, Jews had to sit on separate seats. Children at school were taught to believe in anti-semitic ideas.

In 1935 two laws known as the **Nuremburg Laws** were made against Jews. The first took away their German citizenship. The second forbade marriages between Jews and non-Jews.

After this, violence against Jews increased. Thousands fled to other countries but just as many stayed – and life for them became very hard. In many towns they found it difficult to get food, for grocers and butchers often put up signs in their windows saying 'Jews not admitted'. Sometimes they could not even get milk for their young children. Chemists would not sell them drugs or medicines. Hotels would not give them a night's lodging. And wherever they went, there were mocking signs such as 'Jews Strictly Forbidden To Enter This Town' or 'Jews Enter This Place At Their Own Risk'.

In November 1938 a Jew shot a Nazi official dead. Hitler was furious. He ordered **Himmler**, the SS leader and Police Chief, to begin a week of terror against the Jewish population. This started on 10 November 1938 with the '**Night of Broken Glass**'. Nearly 10,000 Jewish shop keepers had their shop windows smashed and the contents looted. Jewish homes and synagogues went up in flames. Dozens of Jews were killed and thousands arrested.

Worse was to follow. The Jews were ordered to pay

An SA and an SS man together try to stop people from shopping in a Jewish clothes shop

a fine of one billion marks. Jewish men and women were forced to get down on their hands and knees to clean streets with scrubbing brushes. Most worrying of all, Himmler ordered a massive expansion of the concentration camps at Buchenwald, Dachau, Sachsenhausen and Lichtenburg.

The important question to ask and to answer is: how could such terrible things happen in a civilised country such as Germany? Who was to blame? Study the following pieces of evidence and decide for yourself.

A. See picture on the opposite page.

B. A German historian, Ernst Nolte, wrote the following about the SA boycott of Jewish shops:

> 'A committee headed by Julius Streicher appealed to the public for a boycott of Jewish shops and businesses, and on 1 April 1933, members of the SA spent the day on sentry duty in every town and village in Germany, holding placards and challenging citizens . . . not to patronise the businesses of this particular group of their fellow citizens. It was . . . a feast for the cameras and offensive also to the order-loving German people who . . . must have experienced at that moment their first inkling of things to come. The action was hurriedly called off.'

C. An English writer, Christopher Isherwood, who was living in Germany at the time, described the kind of situation which led to acts of brutality against Jews:

> 'Every evening, I sit in the big half-empty artists' cafe by the Memorial church, where the Jews and left-wing intellectuals bend their heads together over the marble tables, speaking in low, scared voices. . . . Almost every evening, the SA men come into the cafe. Sometimes they are only collecting money. Sometimes they have come to make an arrest. One evening a Jewish writer who was present ran into the telephone box to ring up the police. The Nazis dragged him out, and he was taken away. Nobody moved a finger. You could have heard a pin drop, till they were gone. . .'

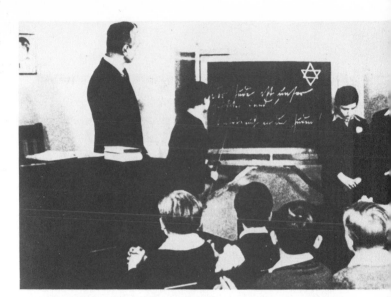

D *1935: two Jewish boys in a German classroom have been made to stand at the front of the class. The writing on the blackboard says 'The Jews are our greatest enemy! Beware of the Jews!' The star is the Star of David, a symbol of the Jewish religion*

E. Shortly after the 'Night of Broken Glass' in 1938, a German citizen wrote this anonymous letter to the British Consul in Cologne:

> 'Cologne, 12 November 1938.
> To the Herr General Konsul,
> I feel the urge to present to you a true report of the recent riots, plunderings and destruction of Jewish businesses, dwellings and burnings of synagogues.
> *The German people have nothing whatever to do with these riots and burnings.*
> Whilst the "angry and excited folk", as the newspapers so well expressed it, still slept . . . the police supplied all available young and newly-enlisted SA men, strengthened by a mob of riff-raff, with axes, housebreaking tools and ladders at the police headquarters. A list of the names and addresses of all Jewish shops and flats was provided and the mob proceeded to do their work under the leadership of SA men. The police had strict orders to remain neutral. . .
> (Signed) A Civil Servant.'

Work section

A. Study source A.
1. What do you think the posters on the window might say?
2. What effect, according to source B, did the posters have on the shoppers?

B. Read source C. Why do you think that nobody in the cafe tried to help the Jewish writer when he was dragged out by the SA?

C. Study source D.
1. Suggest why the schoolteacher has made the two Jewish boys stand at the front of the class.
2. What reasons do you think he might give to the class for saying 'The Jews are our greatest enemy'?

D. According to source E, who was responsible for the 'Night of Broken Glass'?

5

YOUNG PEOPLE IN NAZI GERMANY

A Hitler Youth camp at Nuremburg in the Summer of 1934. Note the loudspeaker on the tower in the centre of the camp

Hitler took great trouble to make sure that young people were loyal to him and to the Nazi Party.

In schools, textbooks were rewritten to paint a good picture of the Nazis. Teachers had to belong to the German Teachers League and were made to put across Nazi ideas in their lessons. To make sure they knew exactly what to do, teachers had to go on compulsory training courses during school holidays.

As a result of such measures, German schoolchildren were not so much educated as indoctrinated. **Indoctrination** means getting people to believe in a set of ideas. You can judge for yourself how this was done at school in this extract from a school mathematics textbook:

> 'A bomber aircraft on take-off carries twelve dozen bombs, each weighing ten kilos. The aircraft takes off for Warsaw, international centre of Jews. It bombs the town. On take-off with all bombs on board and a fuel tank containing 100 kilos of fuel, the aircraft weighed about eight tons. When it returns from the crusade, there are still 230 kilos of fuel left. What is the weight of the aircraft when empty?'

Outside school, young people had to belong to youth organisations which taught them loyalty to Hitler and trained them in military skills. There were five organisations for youngsters to join. Together they made up the **Hitler Youth Movement**:

The Hitler Youth Movement		
Age	*Boys*	*Girls*
6 - 10	The Pimpfen (The Little Fellows)	
10 - 14	The Jungvolk (The Young Folk)	The Jungmadel (Young Girls)
14 - 18	The Hitlerjugend (Hitler Youth – HJ)	The Bund Deutsche Madchen (The German Girls League)

By 1939 some eight million young Germans belonged to the Hitler Youth Movement.

What was the purpose of the youth organisations? Hitler gave one answer to this question when he said:

The Hitler Youth Movement involved girls as much as boys: this group of girls from the German Girls' League is on a day's march as part of the girls' training

'The weak must be chiselled away. I want young men and women who can suffer pain. A young German must be swift as a greyhound, as tough as leather, and as hard as Krupp's steel.'

So when youngsters met in their youth groups they had to do hard physical training. A German mother described the training that her son had to do:

'A twelve mile march was considered nothing for boys who are trained until they can make a march of fifty miles without any food other than the concentrated rations they carry in their packs. Nupp was recovering from a heavy cold but he was not excused the hike. He had a severe relapse as a result. . . Later the the doctor confided to me that often after one of these lengthy marches he had as many as thirty boys in hospital.'

Every year, Hitler Youth Members had to go to training camps where they learned how to read maps, did sports and gymnastics, and were taught Nazi ideas. Camp training was taken very seriously. On one occasion, a fourteen-year-old sentry standing guard at the entrance to a camp shot a ten year old boy who could not remember the password.

Every youngster had a 'performance book' in which marks for athletics, camping and fighting skills were recorded. Those with the best marks were sent to special schools where they were trained to be the leaders of the future. The **Adolf Hitler Schools** took boys from the Jungvolk at the age of twelve and gave them six years of tough training before sending them on to university or the army. The very best of these pupils went on to schools called **Order Castles** where they were stretched to the limits of endurance. At one of them, students were woken in the middle of the night to do open air PT exercises during the winter. They played war games with live ammunition. They washed in an icy stream two kilometres away from their living quarters. Students who were not injured or killed by their training graduated to be the very models of Hitler's idea of youth – swift, tough and very hard.

Work section

A. Why do you think Hitler and the Nazis put so much effort into organising the lives of young people?

B. Study the extract from a school mathematics textbook on the opposite page.
1. In what ways does this extract differ from exercises in your own mathematics textbook?
2. What do you think were the purposes of this exercise?

C. Study the photographs in this chapter carefully. Then, using the information and evidence you have read about young people, write a diary of one day in a Hitler Youth camp.

D. To help you remember what you have read, make revision notes on Chapters 3, 4 and 5. Use points C, D and E of the revision guide on page 20 to help you organise the information clearly.

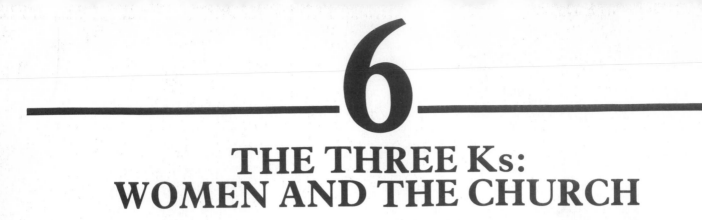

6

THE THREE Ks:
WOMEN AND THE CHURCH

The place of women

Shortly after coming to power in 1933, Hitler made a **Law for the Encouragement of Marriage**. It said that the government would give all newly married couples a loan of 1000 marks – the equivalent of nine months wages. When their first child was born they could keep a quarter of the money. On the birth of their second child they could keep the second quarter. They could keep the third quarter on the birth of a third child, and the entire amount on the birth of a fourth.

Ten years later, in 1943, the Nazi leaders planned another law to encourage people to have children – but this law was very different.

> 'All single and married women up to the age of thirty-five who do not already have four children should be obliged to produce four children by racially pure . . . German men. Whether these men are married is without significance. Every family that already has four children must set the husband free for this action.'

The new law never came into effect, but it shows us exactly what the Nazi leaders thought about women: their job was to bear as many children as possible. Hitler summed it up when he said that women should stick to the '**the three Ks**' – *Kinder, Kirche und Kuche*, Children, Church and Cooking.

Women in Nazi Germany therefore found themselves being forced to stay at home. Within months of Hitler coming to power, many women doctors and civil servants were sacked from their jobs. Then women lawyers and teachers were dismissed. By 1939 there were few women left in professional jobs.

Even at home, women were not free to do as they liked. The Nazi party tried to stop them from following fashions. Make-up and wearing trousers were frowned upon. Hair was to be arranged either in a bun or in plaits, but not dyed or permed. Slimming was discouraged because being slim was not thought to be good for childbearing.

The only thing that women were actively encouraged to do was to have children. Every 12 August, the birthday of Hitler's mother, the Motherhood Cross was awarded to the women who had most children.

The government also set up homes for unmarried mothers. These were called *Lebensborn* – The Spring of Life – and could be recognised by a white flag with a red dot in the middle. The unusual thing about these maternity homes was they were brothels as well. An unmarried woman could go there with the aim of

A Nazi poster of 1937 showing what Nazis thought a woman's role in life should be – a housewife and mother

becoming pregnant and would be introduced to 'racially pure' SS men.

The Nazi Church

Although Hitler said that the church should be part of every woman's life, religion did not prosper under Nazi rule. Read, for example, what happened to Cardinal Innitzer, the Archbishop of Vienna, after he preached an anti-Nazi sermon in church in 1938:

> 'On Saturday evening, the 8th [*October*], at about 7.30 pm, groups of young men belonging to the SA and HJ, but not in party uniform, began to arrive at the Stephansplatz in parties of five, armed with ladders and bludgeons [*clubs*]. The ladders were planted against the cardinal's palace and the lads entered the first floor of the building after smashing in all the windows. Once inside,

A religious procession organised by the National Reich Church

they destroyed every religious picture to be seen . . . smashed the busts of several Popes, stole valuable chalices [*cups*] . . . and collected the robes of the Cardinal . . . which they threw into the courtyard with several items of furniture and set fire to them . . . A similar attack was made on the residence and officers of the dean of the cathedral, and a priest there was actually thrown out of the window and both his legs were broken.'

Protestant as well as Catholic churchmen were badly treated by the Nazis. One Protestant leader, Martin Niemöller, was arrested by the Gestapo after preaching an anti-Nazi sermon, and kept in solitary confinement in a concentration camp for the next seven years.

So what did Hitler mean when he said that the church should be an important part of a woman's life? He was thinking of a new Nazi church, the **National Reich Church**, set up in 1936. Judge for yourself the kind of religion it offered, by reading this extract from its rules:

'In the National Reich Church . . . only national 'Orators of the Reich' will be allowed to speak.

The National Reich Church demands an immediate stop to the printing and sale of the Bible in Germany.

The National Reich Church will remove from the altars of all churches the Bible, the cross and religious objects.

On the altars there must be nothing but *Mein Kampf*, and to the left of this a sword.'

Work section

A. Explain in your own words how the 'Law for the Encouragement of Marriage' tried to encourage married couples to have large families.

B. Read this advertisement which appeared in a German newspaper in 1935:

'52 year-old, pure Aryan physician, fighter at Tannenburg, wishing to settle down, desires male offspring through civil marriage with young, healthy virgin of pure Aryan stock, undemanding, suited to heavy work and thrifty, with flat heels, without earrings, if possible without money. No marriage brokers. Secrecy guaranteed. Letters to box number AEH 151,094. C/o M. Neuest.'

1. Describe in your own words the kind of woman this doctor wanted to marry.
2. For what reasons do you think the doctor wanted to be married?
3. Can you think of a reason why the doctor preferred his future wife to have no money?
4. How likely do you think the doctor was to find a wife through this advertisement?
5. Do you think this advertisement would be allowed in a newspaper today? Explain your answer.

C. Study the photograph above and read the rules of the National Reich Church. Explain in your own words the kind of religion which the Nazis wanted Germans to follow.

7

WORKERS AND WORK IN NAZI GERMANY

When Hitler came to power in 1933, six million Germans were out of work. His most urgent task was to find them jobs, for during the election campaigns he had promised the voters 'work and bread' if he ever became leader.

The RAD

Hitler's first action was to set up a **National Labour Service** (*Reichsarbeitsdienst* or RAD). This organisation gave men jobs in public works schemes – digging drainage ditches on farms, planting new forests, building schools and hospitals. The biggest public works scheme was the building of a network of motorways. Men in the RAD had to wear military uniform and live in camps, and they were given only pocket money as wages. But for many thousands of men, that was better than life with no work at all – and they got free meals.

Men of the National Labour Service march past Hitler in a parade in July 1938

The attack on unemployment

The results of Hitler's attack on unemployment look impressive at first sight:

Unemployment in Germany	
January 1933	6,014,000
January 1934	3,773,000
January 1935	2,974,000
January 1936	2,520,000
January 1937	1,853,000
January 1938	1,052,000
January 1939	302,000

In fact, the drop in unemployment was not all due to the creation of new jobs. As you know, many Jews and women were forced out of their jobs soon after Hitler came to power. Although their jobs were given to unemployed people, the names of the Jews who became unemployed were not then recorded in the unemployment registers.

The most important reason for the fall in unemployment during these years was **rearmament**. As we shall see, Hitler planned to make Germany a strong and independent country, and that meant building up the size and strength of the army. In March 1935 he started **compulsory military service** for young men, and set up an air force. The army quickly grew from 100,000 men in 1933 to 1,400,000 in 1939. Of course, the men doing their military service did not count as unemployed, so this took 1,300,000 off the registers. And to equip this new army, 46 billion marks were spent on weapons and equipment, so many thousands of people were given work in making the tools of war.

Because Hitler wanted a strong, independent Germany, he had to make the country self-sufficient in food and materials. He ordered Germany's scientists to find artificial substitutes for food and materials imported from other countries. They quickly developed all sorts of substitutes; wool and cotton were made from pulped wood, coffee from acorns, petrol from coal, make-up from flour, and so on. As all these things were made in Germany in place of imported goods, many of the unemployed found work in new industries.

The German Labour Front

What was work like for the people who found jobs? One new feature of work in Nazi Germany was that there were no trade unions. Within months of coming to power, Hitler abolished all trade unions and set up the **German Labour Front** in their place. It was run by a former chemist, Doctor Robert Ley. He said this in a speech in 1933, the day after the trade unions were abolished:

'Workers! Your institutions are sacred to us National Socialists. I myself am a poor peasant's son and understand poverty. . . . Workers! I swear to you we will not only keep everything which exists, we will build up the rights and protection of the workers even further.'

Doctor Ley did make some improvements in the life of workers. He made sure, for example, that bosses could not sack workers on the spot. But he also made sure that workers could not leave a job without the government's permission, and that only government-run labour exchanges could arrange new jobs.

Worse, Doctor Ley abolished the right of workers to bargain for higher wages, and he made strikes illegal. He also got rid of the limitations on the number of hours a person could be made to work. By 1939, many Germans found themselves working 60 to 72 hours a week.

Not many workers complained, however. This was not just because they were afraid of what might happen if they did complain. By 1936 the average factory worker was earning 35 marks a week – ten times more than the dole money which six million people were receiving in 1932.

Work section

A. Study this photograph of a motorway in Germany in the 1930s. Make a list of the jobs that are created by this sort of building programme. Before making your list, think about the materials needed for construction as well as about the actual construction work.

B. Study the unemployment figures for 1933 – 9, then answer these questions:
1. Which year shows the greatest fall in unemployment? How do you explain this fall?
2. Which year shows the smallest fall in unemployment? Why do you think this was such a small drop in comparison to previous years?

C. 'History will judge us according to whether we have succeeded in providing work' (Adolf Hitler). What is your judgement? Complete these statements for and against the argument that Hitler succeeded in providing work, then give your opinion.

Successful	Not successful
Before Hitler came to power in 1933, _____ Germans were unemployed. By 1939 only _____ were out of work. This means that Hitler created _____ jobs in seven years.	Many of the jobs that Hitler provided were taken away from _____ and from _____, so he wasn't actually creating new jobs. There were disadvantages in many of the jobs that Hitler created. Men in the RAD were not paid wages: they got only _____ and _____. Workers in factories were not allowed to belong to _____. _____ of the unemployed joined the army to do compulsory military service. Although their names were removed from the unemployment registers, these men did not have jobs.

8

3,740 HOURS: LEISURE IN NAZI GERMANY

Hitler and the Nazi Party aimed to control every part of people's lives, and that included their free time. A huge party organisation called **Strength through Joy** (*Kraft Durch Freude* – KDF) had the job of organising leisure activities for the people.

The KDF was run by Doctor Robert Ley, leader of the German Labour Front. He worked out that there are 8,760 hours in a year, and that the average German spent one third of them sleeping and a quarter of them at work. That left nearly half the time – 3,740

The maiden voyage of a Strength Through Joy liner, the Robert Ley, *1939*

hours – free for leisure. Doctor Ley wanted to be sure that these leisure hours were not wasted: people with nothing to do in their free time would get bored and frustrated, and this would make them into bored and frustrated workers. Happy people with plenty to do in their free time would be more likely to work hard at their jobs.

So Doctor Ley and the KDF drew up massive leisure programmes for working people. The biggest programme provided workers with cheap holidays. Doctor Ley had two 25,000 tonne liners built to take workers on ocean cruises at bargain prices. A cruise to the Canary Islands, for example, cost 62 marks, the equivalent of two weeks' wages. Although most workers could afford this, it was only loyal and hardworking members of the Nazi Party who were given places on the cruise liners.

For those who could not get a place on a cruise ship, there were walking holidays in the mountains for 28 marks a week or, in winter, skiing holidays in Bavaria. The price of 28 marks included travel, board and lodging, the hire of skis, and lessons from an instructor. People with a taste for foreign travel could have two weeks in Switzerland for 65 marks, or a tour of Italy for 155 marks.

The KDF controlled most forms of entertainment. Each year, around seven million people took part in KDF sports matches. The KDF arranged mass outings to the theatre and the opera. It had its own symphony orchestra which toured the country playing music in areas not usually visited by orchestras. It laid on evening classes for adults.

The KDF was also involved in a plan to provide workers with cheap cars. Hitler ordered that a 'People's Car' – a **Volkswagen** – must be built at a price that anyone could afford. It was designed by an Austrian engineer, Ferdinand Porsche, who was told by Hitler that it 'should look like a beetle'.

The price of a 'beetle' was set at 990 marks – the equivalent of thirty-five weeks wages. To help workers buy a car, Doctor Ley started a hire-purchase scheme. Workers paid 5 marks a week until 750 marks were in the bank; then they would be given an order number

entitling them to a car as soon as it was made. In fact, the whole scheme was a swindle. Not a single Volkswagen was made for a German customer. Although workers paid millions of marks into the hire-purchase scheme, the Volkswagen factory was turned into a weapons factory as soon as the Second World War started in 1939.

A poster encouraging workers to save up for a 'Volkswagen'. It says 'You must save five marks a week if you want to ride in your own car'

Work section

A. Look at the photograph of the Strength Through Joy liner, then answer these questions:

1. Where might this liner have been going?
2. What do you think the people in this photograph all had in common?
3. Roughly how much did it cost to go on trips like this?
4. This photograph was taken in 1943; Germany had been at war since 1939. Why do you think the Nazis were building liners like this rather than more warships?
5. For what purpose do you think this photograph was taken? Explain your answer.

B. Read this joke which went around Germany in 1939:

> A car worker at the Volkswagen factory cannot afford to buy his own car, so he steals the pieces one by one, and takes them all home to put together in his garage. When he has all the pieces together, he finds he has built a machine gun carrier.

1. Using the information you have read in this chapter, explain what this joke means.
2. What does this joke tell you about the attitude of German people towards the government?

9

'WINNING PEOPLE OVER': PROPAGANDA AND CENSORSHIP

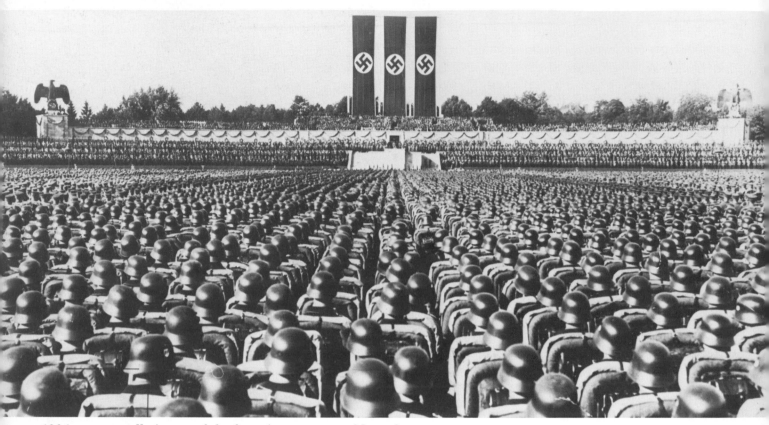

1936: a mass rally in one of the four giant arenas at Nuremburg

One of the most important posts in the Nazi government was held by the man pictured opposite, **Doctor Joseph Goebbels**, Minister of National Enlightenment and Propaganda.

Propaganda

Propaganda is a form of advertising. Its aim is to persuade large numbers of people to think what you want them to think and to believe what you want them to believe. Goebbels' job was to make the Germans believe in Nazi ideas and to be loyal to Hitler and the Party. And it had to be total belief: as Goebbels said in 1937

> 'The essence of propaganda consists in winning people over to an idea so sincerely, so vitally, that in the end they succumb to it utterly and can never escape from it.'

Goebbels used every available method for 'winning people over'. First, he made sure that newspapers printed only stories favourable to the government. Every morning the editors of Berlin's newspapers had to go to the Propaganda Ministry where Goebbels told them what news to print and what the headlines

should be. Newspapers which printed stories he had not approved were closed down.

All Germany's radio stations were under Goebbels' control, so he used the radio to hammer the Nazi message home. He encouraged people to listen to the radio by producing cheap radio sets which most people could afford. The VE radio – the 'People's Receiver' – sold for 76 marks, while the DKE – the 'German Mini Receiver' – cost only 35 marks, about a week's wages. To make sure that people heard the radio when they were not at home, Goebbels had loudspeaker pillars built in the streets, and ordered all cafés to have their radios turned on for important programmes.

Goebbels' most spectacular form of propaganda was the **mass rally**. The most famous of the mass rallies were held in August each year at Nuremburg. A Nuremburg rally lasted a whole week and was held in four specially built arenas outside the town. Just one of these arenas could hold 400,000 people. There they watched army parades and gymnastic displays. They listened to massed choirs, brass bands and to speeches. They looked up at air force fly-pasts and firework displays.

Every event at a rally was staged to perfection. At

the 1937 rally, 100,000 men, each exactly 0.75 metres apart, marched past Hitler carrying 32,000 flags and banners. Above them in the night sky, 150 vertical searchlights created a dome of light that could be seen stabbing into the sky from over 100 kilometres away.

Censorship

Goebbels was a brilliant organiser of propaganda, but he could not trust propaganda alone to win people over. He also had to use censorship to stop other ideas from spreading. Censorship means to ban information or entertainment which the government thinks is harmful.

Every kind of information and entertainment was censored. Jazz music was not allowed at dances because it had its origins among the black people of America. Films were censored for all sorts of reasons: a 'Tarzan' film of 1933 was banned because both Tarzan and Jane were scantily dressed, while a war film about the German navy could not be screened because it showed a sailor drunk. Goebbels even encouraged students to censor books written by Jews or communists by burning them; in 1933, students in Berlin destroyed 20,000 books in a bonfire outside the University of Berlin.

People could not even say things against the Nazis in private. Complaining about the government was against the law. Anti-Nazi jokes were forbidden and the penalty for anti-Hitler jokes was death. A priest who told a joke about Hitler to an electrician working in his church was reported to the Gestapo, taken before a court, and sentenced to death.

Doctor Joseph Goebbels making a speech in 1926

Work section

A. Test your understanding of this chapter by explaining what these words mean: propaganda; rally; censorship.

B. Here are three jokes which were popular in Germany in the late 1930s. One could be told without getting into trouble but the others could not. Which joke do you think was permitted? Explain why the others would not have been allowed.

  1. Hitler is on a fishing holiday with Mussolini, dictator of Italy, and Neville Chamberlain, Prime Minister of Britain. Chamberlain patiently plays out his line, lights his pipe, and within two hours has hauled in a large catch. Then it is Mussolini's turn. He dives headlong into the lake and grabs a big fat pike. When it is Hitler's turn, he orders all the water to be drained out of the lake. Seeing the fish thrashing about on the dry bed of the lake, Chamberlain asks 'Why don't you just scoop them all up?' Hitler replies, 'They have to beg me first'.
  2. Question: What's the difference between Chamberlain and Hitler?
     Answer: One takes a weekend in the country and the other takes a country in a weekend.
  3. An SS guard tells a prisoner in a concentration camp that he has a glass eye which looks exactly like his real one. If the prisoner can guess which eye is the glass eye, his life will be spared: if he cannot, he will be killed. The prisoner makes the correct guess and when the amazed SS man asks him how he managed it, the prisoner replies: 'I chose the eye with a kindly look in it'.

C. Look through all the pictures in this book. Are there any which you think Goebbels would not have allowed the newspapers to print? Explain why you think he would not have allowed the pictures you have chosen.

D. To help you remember what you have read in the last few chapters, make revision notes on Chapters 6 to 9. Use points F to J of the revision guide on page 20 to help you organise the information clearly.

Revision guide to Part One

This revision guide is an outline of the main points. It is not a set of notes to be copied. You should make your own notes under the sub-headings suggested.

A. Adolf Hitler
1. His life up to 1933
2. His ideas
3. His appeal

B. How Hitler established his dictatorship
1. The election campaign of March 1933
2. Results of the election
3. The Enabling Law, March 1933
4. The take-over of local governments
5. The banning of trade unions
6. The 'Night of the Long Knives', 1934
7. Hitler becomes Fuehrer, 1934
8. The army's oath of loyalty

C. The Nazi police state
1. Himmler and Heydrich
2. The methods of the Gestapo
3. Concentration camps

D. Jews in Nazi Germany
1. Hitler's anti-semitic ideas
2. The dismissal of Jews from jobs, 1933
3. The Nuremburg Laws, 1935
4. The 'Night of Broken Glass', 1938
5. Violence against Jews

E. Young people in Nazi Germany
1. Schools and indoctrination
2. The Hitler Youth Movement
3. Adolf Hitler Schools and Order Castles

F. Women in Nazi Germany
1. The 'three Ks'
2. Restrictions on women
3. The encouragement of childbearing

G. Religion in Nazi Germany
1. The persecution of churchmen
2. The National Reich Church

H. Work in Nazi Germany
1. The National Labour Service
2. The creation of new jobs
3. The German Labour Front

I. Leisure in Nazi Germany

J. Propaganda and censorship
1. Doctor Goebbels
2. Newspapers
3. Radio
4. Mass rallies
5. Censorship

Revision exercise

Read this extract from a newspaper article written by David Lloyd George, one of Britain's greatest politicians and Prime Minister from 1916 to 1922. It appeared in the *Daily Express* in November 1936, fourteen years after he had lost office. Then answer the questions beneath.

> 'I TALKED TO HITLER
> I have just returned from a visit to Germany. . . . I have now seen the famous German leader and also something of the great change he has effected. Whatever one may think of his methods – and they are certainly not those of a parliamentary country – there can be no doubt that he has achieved a marvellous transformation in the spirit of the people, in their attitude toward each other, and in their social and economic outlook. . . . One man has accomplished this miracle. He is a born leader of men. . . . He is the national Leader. . . He is also securing them against the constant dread of starvation which is one of the most poignant memories of the last years of the war and the first years of the peace.'

1. In your own words explain what Lloyd George's opinion of Hitler was.
2. List the things which Lloyd George might have seen in Nazi Germany to make him believe that Hitler had 'achieved a marvellous transformation'.
3. (a) What did Lloyd George mean when he wrote that Hitler's methods were 'certainly not those of a parliamentary country'?
   (b) List the methods that he might have had in mind when he wrote this.
4. Many people disagreed with Lloyd George's opinion of Nazi Germany. Write your own newspaper article under the heading 'I talked to Hitler', giving an unfavourable view of Nazi Germany.

PART
TWO
HITLER AND EUROPE

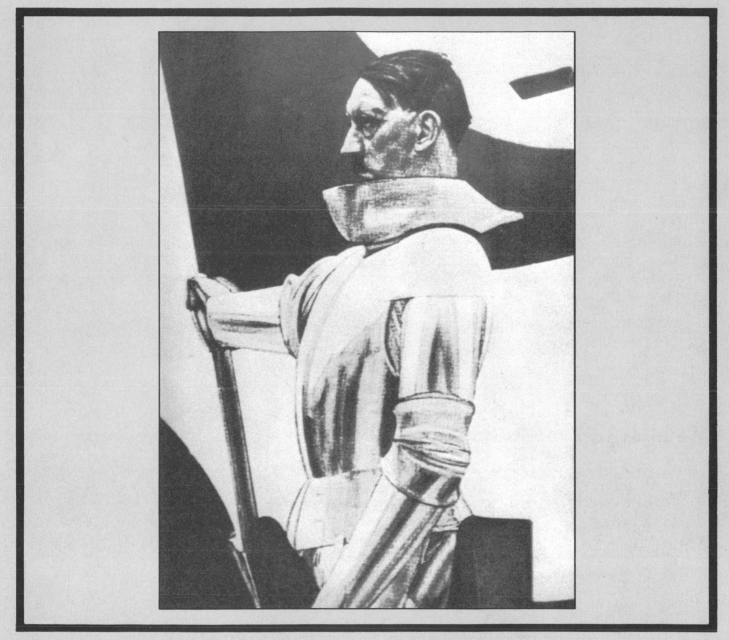

A propaganda poster of 1936: Hitler is shown as an armoured knight setting out on a crusade

You have found out that life in Germany changed enormously during the years 1933 – 9. Hitler set up a dictatorship which gave him total control over the lives of sixty million people. But what was the point of it all? Where was Germany heading?

A secret message written by Hitler in 1936 gives us one answer to this question. It was written to his second-in-command, Herman Goering, who was in charge of the country's economic affairs. The message ended:

'I thus set the following task:

1. The German army must be ready to fight within 4 years.
2. The German economy must be fit for war within 4 years.'

Exactly four years later Germany *was* at war, and had already defeated nine countries in Europe.

Part Two of this book explains why Hitler led Germany down the road to war, and shows how the war which he began destroyed millions of lives and ruined most of Europe.

UNDOING THE TREATY OF VERSAILLES

1936: the German army marches across the River Rhine into the city of Cologne, breaking the Treaty of Versailles

Hitler's aims

Hitler had three main aims in preparing Germany for war. First, he aimed to tear up the **Treaty of Versailles** which brought an end to the Great War of 1914 – 18. This treaty blamed Germany for starting the war, took away huge amounts of land, money and materials from her, and cut her armed forces to the bare minimum. Hitler said:

> 'The Treaty of Versailles is engraved on the minds and hearts of the German people and burned into them. Sixty million people will find their souls aflame with a feeling of rage and shame. Then the people will join in a common cry: "We will have arms again".'

Hitler's second aim was to unite all Germans in a single country. As there were millions of Germans living in neighbouring Austria, Czechoslovakia and Poland, these countries would have to be brought under his control.

His third aim was to provide Germany with what he called *lebensraum*, or 'living space'. Germany was overcrowded, he said, and did not have enough food or raw materials for her needs. The solution was to take over the rich farmlands and mines of countries to the east, particularly Russia and Poland.

All three of these aims could only be achieved if Germany rearmed, massively increasing her armed forces.

Rearmament

In 1934, only a year after coming to power, Hitler gave top secret orders for the armed forces to expand. The army was to treble from 100,000 to 300,000 men. The navy was to build two 'pocket battleships' and six submarines. Hermann Goering was to create an air force and secretly train pilots in civilian flying clubs. These were all forbidden by the Treaty of Versailles.

In 1935 Hitler cast off the cloak of secrecy and announced in public that there would be compulsory military service and that the army would be built up to 550,000 men. The countries around Germany were alarmed and quickly began making alliances with each other in case Germany attacked one of them. Three countries, Britain, France and Italy, signed an agreement condemning Hitler's announcement. But no country took military action to stop this breach of the Treaty of Versailles.

The Rhineland

In 1936 Hitler ordered his army to march into the Rhineland (see map on page 24). The Treaty of Versailles forbade the German army from going within 50 kilometres of the River Rhine, so Hitler's order was a deliberate challenge to this treaty.

It was also a wild gamble, Britain and France had agreed ten years earlier that they would use their armies to stop German troops from entering the Rhineland. Worse, Hitler had only 30,000 fully-equipped troops to send in. As he admitted later, 'If the French had then marched into the Rhineland, we would have had to withdraw with our tails between our legs.'

But the gamble paid off. The British refused to help the French, and the French did not want to fight Germany single-handed. So the German army stayed in the Rhineland and was able to build up a great line of forts on the border with France and Belgium. The building of this so-called 'West Wall' meant that, in future, France and Britain could not easily take military action against Germany if Hitler broke the Treaty of Versailles again.

Alliances

As well as remilitarising the Rhineland in 1936, Hitler made a number of foreign alliances. When a civil war began in Spain, he sent his best air force unit, the Condor Legion, to fight on the side of the nationalist General Franco. If Franco won the war, Hitler would have Spain as an ally. The war also gave the Condor Legion the chance to try out methods of bombing towns from the air.

Hitler also made an agreement in 1936 with Benito Mussolini, dictator of Italy, that they would work closely together in foreign affairs. This agreement was called the **Rome-Berlin Axis** pact and gave Hitler a powerful ally in Europe. An agreement with Japan, the **Anti-Comintern Pact**, gave him an ally on the other side of the world.

Anschluss with Austria

By 1938 Hitler felt strong enough to plan a union, or **anschluss**, with Austria. This was part of his aim to unite all German-speaking people in one country, but it was forbidden by the Treaty of Versailles. He therefore had to be very careful about how he went about it.

Hitler began by ordering the Austrian Nazi Party to make as much trouble as it could. The Austrian Nazis held parades and marches, set buildings on fire, let off bombs, organised fights. When the Austrian government banned them because of this, Hitler held a meeting with the Austrian leader, Kurt Schuschnigg. Hitler threatened to invade Austria unless Schuschnigg gave all the important jobs in his government to Nazis. Schuschnigg had to agree to do this, even though it would mean an Austrian government which was pro-German, pro-Nazi and which would do what Hitler wanted. He tried to get round the problem by holding a plebiscite, or vote, among the Austrian people to see whether they wanted to join with Germany or to stay independent. Hitler feared that the Austrians would vote for independence, so he moved his army to the border to scare Schuschnigg into calling off the plebiscite.

Schuschnigg asked Italy, Britain and France to protect his country, but all three refused. He had to resign. An Austrian Nazi, Seyss-Inquart, took his place as leader, and immediately asked Hitler to send the German army into Austria to 'restore order'.

So Hitler was now able to send his army into Austria by invitation! Strictly speaking, he had not attacked or invaded the country. But behind the army came the SS and the Gestapo to deal with opponents of the Nazis. Schuschnigg quickly found himself being made to clean public toilets, while Austria's Jews were made to get down and scrub streets on their hands and knees. Before long they would all be in concentration camps, while the rest of the Austrian people lived under a Nazi reign of terror.

Work section

A. Test your understanding of what you have read by explaining what these words mean: rearmament; remilitarisation; *anschluss*.

B. Explain how Hitler broke the Treaty of Versailles in each of the following years: 1934; 1935; 1936; 1938.

FROM CZECHOSLOVAKIA TO POLAND

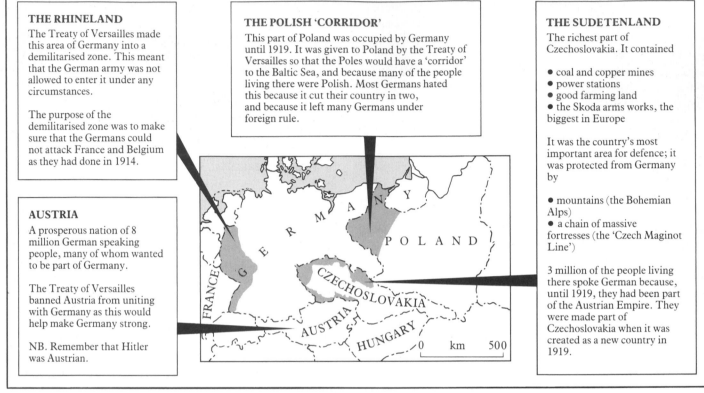

THE RHINELAND
The Treaty of Versailles made this area of Germany into a demilitarised zone. This meant that the German army was not allowed to enter it under any circumstances.

The purpose of the demilitarised zone was to make sure that the Germans could not attack France and Belgium as they had done in 1914.

AUSTRIA
A prosperous nation of 8 million German speaking people, many of whom wanted to be part of Germany.

The Treaty of Versailles banned Austria from uniting with Germany as this would help make Germany strong.

NB. Remember that Hitler was Austrian.

THE POLISH 'CORRIDOR'
This part of Poland was occupied by Germany until 1919. It was given to Poland by the Treaty of Versailles so that the Poles would have a 'corridor' to the Baltic Sea, and because many of the people living there were Polish. Most Germans hated this because it cut their country in two, and because it left many Germans under foreign rule.

THE SUDETENLAND
The richest part of Czechoslovakia. It contained

* coal and copper mines
* power stations
* good farming land
* the Skoda arms works, the biggest in Europe

It was the country's most important area for defence; it was protected from Germany by

* mountains (the Bohemian Alps)
* a chain of massive fortresses (the 'Czech Maginot Line')

3 million of the people living there spoke German because, until 1919, they had been part of the Austrian Empire. They were made part of Czechoslovakia when it was created as a new country in 1919.

The land that Hitler wanted

The Sudetenland crisis

Look at the map above and study the shape of Germany after its union with Austria. Study also the shape of Czechoslovakia; it is rather like a carrot half-buried in the side of Germany. Hitler decided in 1938 to lop off the buried part of the carrot and to make it part of Germany.

He began by peeling off the skin of the Czech carrot – an area called the Sudetenland. Over three million people in this part of Czechoslovakia were German, and most of them supported a Nazi-style party called the Sudeten German Party. Its leader, a PE teacher named **Konrad Henlein**, was in Hitler's pay, and ready to do whatever Hitler told him.

Hitler instructed Henlein to stir up trouble in the Sudetenland. Obediently Henlein arranged riots and demonstrations, and complained that the Czech government was treating the Sudeten Germans unfairly. Meanwhile Hitler ordered his army to get ready to invade Czechoslovakia. When the army moved in, he would make the excuse that it was only there to stop the riots and demonstrations.

Hitler's plan quickly went wrong. The Czechs found out that the German army was gathering on their border, and immediately got ready to fight. They had a big army and strong defences and they also had a powerful ally to help them, France. Hitler had to call off his invasion for the time being: his army was not strong enough to fight two countries at the same time.

Hitler got a second chance to invade Czechoslovakia within months, and he was given the chance by **Neville Chamberlain**, Prime Minister of Britain. Chamberlain thought that the Sudetenland should belong to Germany and persuaded the French to agree with him. He believed that there would be a big war if Hitler did not get what he wanted, a war in which France and Britain would be involved. He was prepared to go to almost any lengths to avoid such a war. This policy was called **appeasement**.

Hitler could now plan for an invasion again without having to worry about the French. So Henlein stirred up even more trouble in the Sudetenland, with the result that Czech police shot a number of Germans. Hitler threatened the Czechs with war again.

The Munich Conference

Neville Chamberlain was still determined to prevent war, so he asked Hitler if he could meet him in Germany to discuss a peaceful solution to the problem. Hitler agreed. During September 1938, Chamberlain

1939: Czech civilians and policemen watch German troops occupy their capital, Prague

flew three times to see Hitler in southern Germany. The third and last meeting was in Munich. The leaders of France and Italy were there too. After much discussion the four men at the Munich Conference agreed that Germany should have the Sudetenland. The Czech leader was not even consulted about this, but he had to accept the decision: Britain and France had taken Germany's side, so the Czechs had no ally to protect them. Hitler, however, promised that he would not threaten any more countries.

Chamberlain flew back to London feeling very pleased with himself. His policy of 'appeasement' seemed to have avoided war. But just six months later, in March 1939, the German army marched into the rest of Czechoslovakia and made the western half if it into part of Germany. Hungary and Poland grabbed the rest. Czechoslovakia had ceased to exist.

Poland

It was now obvious that Hitler was going to grab more land, despite his promise at the Munich Conference. It was also obvious that his next target would be Poland.

As you can see from the map opposite, Germany was divided into two by the '**Polish Corridor**'. Hitler's Germany would not be complete until the Polish Corridor was in his hands. The British and French realised that Hitler would stop at nothing to achieve this so they stopped trying to 'appease' him. They agreed that they would fight to protect Poland.

This should have stopped Hitler. The British and French were against him while, on the other side of Poland lay Russia, Hitler's hated enemy. If Germany attacked Poland, Germany herself would be attacked by three powerful countries.

Hitler got round this problem in a single move which astounded Europe. In August 1939 he made an agreement with the Russians that Germany and Russia would not fight each other. They also secretly agreed to attack Poland and divide it between them. This **Nazi-Soviet Pact** meant that Hitler could invade the Polish Corridor without worrying about Russia.

Early in the morning of 1 September 1939, German tanks rolled across the Polish frontier. Britain and France declared war on Germany two days later. A second world war was about to begin.

Work section

A. Study the expressions on the faces of the Czechs in the photograph above. Notice the clenched fists. Imagine you are one of these people, and write a letter to a friend in another country explaining what has happened. In your letter, try to explain your feelings about the French and British as well as about the Germans.

B. 1. What was the Nazi-Soviet Pact of 1939?
2. Why do you think people were surprised by it?

C. Before going any further, make revision notes on what you have read so far about Hitler and Europe. Use points A to H of the revision guide on page 32 to help you organise the information.

12

THE NAZI CONQUEST OF EUROPE, 1939 – 1941

Hitler's armies invaded Poland on 1 September 1939. By the end of the month they had occupied the capital Warsaw, and had divided the country up with Russia. Hitler's Germany was now complete.

This was not the end of his ambitions, however. His next aim was to take over land in eastern Europe and Russia in order to get *lebensraum* – living space– for Germany. But first he had to deal with France and Britain who had promised to defend Poland. During the spring of 1940, German armies invaded Denmark, Norway, Holland, Belgium, Luxemburg and France. By June, all six countries had been defeated and occupied by the Germans. Britain came under attack next. Only the courage of her fighter pilots during the '**Battle of Britain**' prevented the Germans from sending an invasion fleet across the English Channel.

Realising that Britain could not be beaten easily, Hitler turned his forces to the east, first invading Greece, then Yugoslavia. Finally, in June 1941, he turned on Russia, the old enemy with whom he had made the Nazi-Soviet pact two years before. By December 1941 German armies had captured all western Russia and the Ukraine. As the map below

shows, Hitler was Fuehrer of nearly all Europe by the end of 1941.

What was Hitler's purpose? Where was he taking Germany now? The following documents give us several answers to these questions.

A. 'When this war is ended Germany will set to work in earnest. A great "Awake" will sound throughout the country. Then the German Nation will stop making cannons and will start on the new work of reconstruction for the millions. . . . Out of this work will grow the great German *Reich* of which great poets have dreamed.' (Speech by Hitler, December 1940)

Reich meant Empire, and the countries which Hitler had conquered were to be its colonies. This is what he had in mind:

B. 'What India is for England, the territories of Russia will be for us. If only I could make the German people understand what this space means for our future! . . . The German colonist ought

The defeat of France, June 1940. German troops march through the Arc de Triomphe in Paris

European countries under Hitler's control by the end of 1941

to live on handsome, spacious farms. The German services will be lodged in marvellous buildings, the Governors in palaces. . . . Around the cities, to a depth of 30 or 40 kilometres, we will have a belt of handsome villages connected by the best roads.' (From Hitler's *Table Talk*, August 1941)

What about the non-German people living in these colonies? What could they expect?

C. 'Farm workers . . . no longer have the right to complain, and thus no complaints will be accepted . . . Visiting church is strictly prohibited . . . Visits to theatres, motion pictures or other cultural entertainments are strictly prohibited. Sexual intercourse with women and girls is strictly prohibited . . . Farm workers have to labour as long as demanded by the employer. There are no limits to working time. Every employer has the right to give corporal punishment to his farm workers.' (Nazi Directive: *The Treatment of Foreign Farm Workers*, March 1941)

Workers of any 'non-Aryan' race, particularly Jews and Slavs, were to be worked to death in the 'great German Reich':

D. 'The Slavs are to work for us. In so far as we don't need them, they may die. Therefore compulsory vaccination and German health services are unnecessary. The fertility of the Slavs is undesirable. They may use contraceptives or practise abortion, the more the better. Education is dangerous. It is enough if they can count up to one hundred. Every educated person is a future enemy. . . As for food they won't get any more than is absolutely necessary. We are the masters. We come first.' (Letter written by Martin Bormann, Hitler's deputy, 1941)

Russians were not to be spared, whatever their race:

E. 'The Fuehrer has decided to have Leningrad wiped off the face of the earth. The further existence of this large city [*population three million*] is of no interest once Soviet Russia has been overthrown. . . . The intention is to close in on the city and raze it to the ground by artillery and continuous air attack. . . . The problem of the survival of the population and of supplying it with food is one which cannot and should not be solved by us. In this war for existence we have no interest in keeping even part of this great city's population.' (Order from Hitler, September 1941)

Finally, in Hitler's 'great German Reich', there was to be no place for Jews. In 1939 Himmler and Heydrich, the SS leaders, set up **'Special Action Groups'** (*Einsatzgruppen*) to follow the German armies into Poland. Their job was to round up Jewish families and communities, and put them in **ghettos**. In these walled-off areas of towns, the Jews slowly starved to death or were killed by diseases. The Special Action Groups also followed the armies into Russia in 1941. What they did is described here by a former leader of one of these groups:

F. 'The *Einsatz* unit would enter a village or town and order the prominent Jewish citizens to call together all Jews for the purposes of "resettlement" [*moving to new homes*]. They were asked to hand over their valuables and shortly before execution to surrender their outer clothing. They were taken to the place of executions, usually an anti-tank ditch, in trucks. . . . Then they were shot, kneeling or standing, by firing squads in a military manner and the corpses thrown into the ditch.' (Otto Ohlendorf, speaking at his trial for war crimes in 1946)

As we shall see, this was the first stage of what leading Nazis called 'the final solution of the Jewish Problem'.

Work section

A. Study source B. What sort of life could German colonists look forward to in the 'great German Reich'?

B. Study sources C and D. Then divide a page into two columns.
  1. In one column write down all the things that foreign workers were made to do by the Germans.
  2. In the other column write down all the things that foreign workers were not allowed to do by the Germans.
  3. Suggest as many reasons as you can why the Germans treated foreign workers so badly.

C. Read source E carefully.
  1. Explain in your own words what Hitler intended to do to the city of Leningrad.
  2. Judging by what you have read of Hitler's ideas, why do you think Hitler gave this order?

D. Hitler once said that his 'Reich' would last for 1000 years. Imagine that it is still in existence today and that Britain is part of it. Using the evidence you have read in this chapter and in other parts of the book, write a few paragraphs describing what you think:
  1. Life in Germany would be like; and
  2. What life in Britain would be like.

13
THE FINAL SOLUTION

In January 1942, when most of Europe and much of Russia was under Nazi rule, fifteen leading Nazis met for a secret conference in **Wannsee**, a suburb of Berlin. There they discussed what they called the **'final solution of the Jewish Problem'**. The results of the decisions made at the Wannsee Conference were later described by Rudolf Höss, commander of several concentration camps, during his trial for war crimes in 1946:

> 'The "final solution" of the Jewish question meant the complete extermination of all Jews in Europe. I was ordered to establish extermination facilities at Auschwitz in June 1941. At that time there were already in . . . Poland three other extermination camps; Belzec, Treblinka and Wolzek. . . .
>
> I visited Treblinka to find out how they carried out their extermination. The camp commandant at Treblinka told me he had liquidated 80,000 in the course of half a year. . . .
>
> He used monoxide gas and I did not think his methods were very efficient. So when I set up the extermination building at Auschwitz, I used Zyklon B, which was a crystallised Prussic acid which we dropped into the death chamber from a small opening. It took from three to fifteen minutes to kill all the people in the death chamber, depending on climatic conditions. We knew when the people were dead because their screaming stopped. We usually waited about half an hour before we opened the doors and removed the bodies. After the bodies were removed our special commandos took off the rings and extracted the gold from the teeth of the corpses.
>
> Another improvement we made over Treblinka was that we built our gas chambers to accommodate 2000 people at one time, whereas at Treblinka their ten gas chambers only accommodated 200 people each.'

Between 1942 and 1945 some four and a half million died in the extermination camps. But, as you have already found out, Jews were already being killed in the concentration camps set up before the war, and were being shot by Einsatz units in Russia. In all, the Nazis slaughtered six million Jews.

Jewish boys being taken from their homes to an extermination camp

The lavatory hut at Auschwitz

How was any of this possible? Why did nobody protest or rebel against what was happening? For a start, the Jews did not usually know what was going to happen to them until it was too late. The American writer, William Shirer, explains:

'None of the captives . . . realised what was in store for them. In fact some of them were given pretty picture postcards . . . to be signed and sent back home to their relatives with a printed inscription saying: "We are doing very well here. We have work and we are well treated. We await your arrival."

The gas chambers themselves and the adjoining crematoria, viewed from a short distance, were not sinister-looking places at all. . . . Over them were well kept lawns with flower borders; the signs at the entrances merely said BATHS. The unsuspecting Jews thought they were simply being taken to the baths for the de-lousing that was customary at all camps. And taken to the accompaniment of sweet music!

For there was light music. An orchestra of "young and pretty girls all dressed in white blouses and navy-blue skirts", as one survivor remembered, had been formed from among the inmates. . . .

To such music . . . the men, women and children were led into the "bath houses" where they were told to undress preparatory to taking a "shower". Sometimes they were even given towels. Once they were inside the "shower room" – and perhaps this was the first moment they realised something was amiss, for as many as two thousand were packed into the chamber like sardines, making it difficult to take a bath – the massive door was slid shut, locked and hermetically sealed.'

And what about the Germans themselves? Why did they do nothing to stop the killing? Historians have many answers to this question: people did not know it was happening because the extermination camps were a closely-guarded secret; people were too scared to complain; people who did ask what was happening were told that the camps were false rumours spread by the British. But perhaps another answer is that the Germans had been trained by Nazi propaganda to treat Jews as if they were not human beings. As one historian, Richard Grunberger, puts it:

'As far as the great majority were concerned, Jewish suffering affected beings in another galaxy rather than inhabitants of the same planet as themselves. . . . The holocaust [*the extermination of the Jews*] was not a real event for most Germans, not because it occurred in wartime and under conditions of secrecy, but because Jews were astronomically remote and not real people.'

Work section

A. Rudolf Höss, the commandant of Auschwitz, said at his trial in 1946:

'Let the public continue to regard me as the bloodthirsty beast, the cruel sadist and the mass murderer; for the masses could never imagine the commandant of Auschwitz in any other light. They could never understand that he, too, had a heart and that he was not evil.'

1. Judging by the evidence you have studied in this chapter, explain in detail why Rudolf Höss can be considered 'evil'.
2. Suggest why he thought he was not evil, despite the things he did at Auschwitz.

THE END OF HITLER'S EUROPE, 1942 – 1945

May 1945: Russian soldiers on top of the Reichstag building in Berlin

At the end of 1941 Hitler ruled most of Europe. A little over three years later he was dead, his armies were beaten and his Reich lay in ruins. How did this happen?

Turning points

In December 1941 the USA went to war with Japan after Japanese planes bombed the American fleet at **Pearl Harbour** in the Pacific Ocean. As Japan was one of Germany's allies, Hitler declared war on the United States.

This was a fatal mistake. America was rich and strong. She could not only send huge armies to fight both Germany and Japan but could also give help to Britain and Russia, the only European countries still fighting Germany.

With American money and help, the Russians were able to form a new army. For five months in 1942 they fought a massive battle against the Germans in the city of **Stalingrad**. Hitler refused to order a retreat even when it became clear that his armies were beaten. Over 80,000 Germans died in battle, and 90,000 of them surrendered. Only 5,000 of them ever returned from captivity.

While one German army was dying in the snows of Russia, another was on the run in the deserts of North Africa. At the battle of **El Alamein** in Egypt, a British army defeated the German Afrika Korps and drove it entirely out of Africa.

The battles at Stalingrad and El Alamein were turning points in the war in Europe. From then on the Germans were defeated in one great battle after another. In 1943 American and British forces invaded

Europe through Italy and in June 1944 they landed in France on 'D-Day'. In the east, the Russian armies steadily drove the Germans back out of their country. And all the while, British and American bomber planes were making raids on German cities, pounding them into rubble and killing many thousands of civilians.

The Generals' Plot of 20 July 1944

By the summer of 1944 the German armies were retreating in France, Italy and Russia. A group of German army generals realised that Germany could never win the war. They plotted to kill Hitler: and once he was dead they intended to make peace.

On 20 July 1944, Colonel von Stauffenberg, leader of the plotters, attended a meeting held by Hitler at his headquarters near Berlin. At the meeting were twenty-four officers, busy drawing up war plans. In his brief-case Stauffenberg had a time-bomb. Soon after the meeting began, he made an excuse to leave the room and went outside. Ten minutes later he heard the roar of his bomb exploding in the crowded room. Then he flew to Berlin where he announced that Hitler was dead and that the army generals were taking power in his place.

Stauffenberg had spoken too soon. Although the bomb had killed four men in the conference room, Hitler was still alive. His hair was singed, his ear-drums broken and his clothes in shreds, but he was not seriously injured. And he was determined to get revenge.

It took the Gestapo only a few hours to capture Stauffenberg and the other plotters. After a short trial they were executed by being hung from meat hooks on piano wire.

The end of Hitler's Reich

Although the Generals' Plot had failed, Hitler knew he could no longer trust the army. This did not stop him from ordering his troops to fight to the death. But for the next nine months it could do nothing but retreat as the British, Americans and Russians closed in on Germany. Hitler accused the army of treachery.

At the start of 1945 Hitler took to living in a large concrete bunker 15 metres deep in the ground beneath

The conference room after the explosion

the Chancellery in Berlin. There he lost touch with the realities of the outside world. He sent out orders to armies which no longer existed. He ordered that all Germany's factories, power stations and communications must be destroyed to stop them falling into the hands of the enemy.

In April 1945 the Russian army entered Berlin. Hitler at last realised what his generals had known a year before – Germany could not win the war. But rather than surrender he decided to commit suicide.

Living with him in the bunker were Goebbels and his family, and Eva Braun, a woman who had loved him for many years and who now wanted to die with him. On 29 April they were married. Early the next morning Hitler shot himself and Eva took poison. Their bodies were then carried into a small garden above the bunker, soaked with petrol, and burned. The day after that, Goebbels and his wife also took their lives after having their five children poisoned.

Hitler's Reich lasted for only another week. Admiral Doenitz of the German navy became leader in Hitler's place, but there was nothing left to lead. On 7 May 1945 Germany surrendered to the Allied invaders, bringing the war in Europe to an end.

Work section

A. In his book '*The Rise and Fall of the Third Reich*', William Shirer wrote that Hitler's decision to go to war with the USA was 'one of his monumental miscalculations'.

1. For what reasons can Hitler's declaration of war on America be described as a great mistake?
2. If Hitler had not declared war on America, do you think the outcome of the Second World War might have been different? Explain your answer.

B. Do you think that General von Stauffenberg was right to try to kill Hitler on 20 July 1944? If the plot had succeeded do you think the course of events in history since 1944 would have been different? Explain your answer.

C. Make revision notes on Chapters 12 – 14, using the guide on the next page to help you.

Revision Guide to Part Two

As before, you should use these note headings as a framework for your own notes on what you have read about Hitler and Europe.

A. Hitler's foreign policy aims
1. The Treaty of Versailles
2. The union of all Germans in Germany
3. The conquest of *lebensraum*

B. Hitler's rearmament of Germany

C. The remilitarisation of the Rhineland, 1936

D. Hitler's alliances
1. The Rome-Berlin Axis, 1936
2. The Anti-Comintern Pact, 1936
3. Help for Franco in the Spanish Civil War, 1936 – 9

E. The Anschluss with Austria, 1938

F. The take-over of Czechoslovakia, 1938 – 9
1. The Sudetenland Crisis, 1938
2. The Munich Conference, 1938
3. The invasion of Czechoslovakia, 1939

G. The Nazi-Soviet Pact, 1939

H. The invasion of Poland, 1939

I. The conquest of Europe, 1939 – 41

J. Hitler's 'Reich'

K. The 'Final Solution'
1. The Einsatzgruppen in Russia
2. The Wannsee Conference
3. The extermination camps

L. The defeat of Hitler's Europe
1. War with the USA
2. The Battle of Stalingrad, 1942
3. The Battle of El Alamein, 1942
4. British and American attacks on Europe, 1943 – 4
5. The Generals' Plot of 1944
6. The fall of Berlin, 1945
7. The death of Hitler

Revision Exercise

Read this comment made by the German historian, Joachim C. Fest, on Hitler's life and career:

> 'Hitler was undoubtably great and a figure of historic significance. There is tragedy here too; the tragedy is that of his victims, and the greatness stems almost exclusively from destructiveness. In the sum total of his life, constructive achievements are lacking to an extent scarcely paralleled among the most savage figures of history.'

Judging by what you have learned from this book, give answers to these questions:

1. What do you think Joachim Fest meant by 'constructive achievements'?
2. (a) Do you think it is fair to say that in Hitler's life, 'constructive achievements are lacking'?
   (b) Can you think of any constructive achievements in Hitler's career which would make you disagree with Joachim Fest? Explain your answer in detail.
3. (a) What do you think Joachim Fest means by the 'tragedy' of Hitler's victims?
   (b) List as many kinds of 'victims' as you can.

4. Do you agree that Hitler was 'great'? Before answering, try to decide what makes a historical figure 'great'. Then explain your answer in detail.